A Pocketful of Passage

GREAT LAKES BOOKS
*A complete listing of the books in this series
can be found online at wsupress.wayne.edu*

A Pocketful of Passage

LORAINE CAMPBELL

Illustrations by Marie L. Campbell

Wayne State University Press
Detroit

Library of Congress Cataloging-in-Publication Data
Campbell, Loraine.
A pocketful of Passage / Loraine Campbell ;
illustrations by Marie L. Campbell.
p. cm. — (Great Lakes books)
ISBN-13: 978-0-8143-3341-9 (pbk. : alk. paper)
ISBN-10: 0-8143-3341-9 (pbk. : alk. paper)
1. Bowen family—Juvenile literature. 2. Passage Island Lighthouse
(Isle Royale, Mich.)—Juvenile literature. 3. Lighthouse keepers—Family
relationships—Michigan—Isle Royale—Juvenile literature. 4. Bowen,
Vernon, 1899—Juvenile literature. 5. Hoge, Ann Bowen, 1933—
Juvenile literature. I. Title.
VK1139.C35 2007
387.1'550922774997—dc22
[B]
2006031686

Designed and typeset by Maya Rhodes
Composed in Kidprint MT and ITC Clearface

*In memory of Annie, who generously shared her memories,
and for my mother and father,
who instilled in me a great love of the Great Lakes.*

Contents

vii

$\mathcal{A}$ Note to the Reader

The Great Lakes are huge, beautiful, and ever changing freshwater seas. For hundreds of years people have explored their shores, harvested fish from their depths, and used them as transportation routes. Schooners, steam ships, and modern freighters have sailed the deep waters of Lake Superior, down through the St. Marys River and the locks at Sault Ste. Marie. From Lakes Huron and Michigan, ships traveled through Lakes Erie and Ontario, on through the St. Lawrence Seaway and all the way to the Atlantic Ocean.

The Great Lakes lap the shores of eight American states, but Michigan is the only state bordered by four of the five Great Lakes. Look at any United States map and you will see that Michigan's Lower Peninsula looks like a big mitten floating in a sea of blue. The state's Upper Peninsula is sandwiched between Lakes Michigan and Huron on the south, and mighty Lake Superior on the north. Michigan has more than 3,200 miles of Great Lakes shoreline. It also has more lighthouses than any other state in the country.

Most of the Great Lakes lighthouses were built in the 1800s, long before satellites and computerized navigation aids were invented. Ships' crews learned the flash patterns and colors of each beacon and used these visual markers to steer their vessels away from dangerous rocks, into the deep shipping channels, and through dangerous storms.

In 1881 the United States government built a lighthouse on the southern tip of tiny Passage Island, located off the northeast tip of Isle Royale in northern Lake Superior. Passage Island was named for the deep, three-mile passage between it and Isle Royale. That narrow shipping channel is the safest route for ships and a shortcut past miles of dangerous rocks farther east. The lighthouse was built on a rocky bluff high above the passage. It was made with black and brown fieldstones that matched the dark, rough rocks below it. However, the top of the forty-foot tower was painted snow-white and gleamed brightly for all to see. More than fifty men lived in the sturdy stone house over the years.

Until the 1950s, lighthouse keepers and their families lived at lighthouse stations and tended the signals. Later, as radar and other technologies were developed, the United States Coast Guard removed the keepers and operated the lights by solar power and remote control. Some stations were abandoned because they were considered unnecessary. When lighthouses no longer required human attendants, the lighthouse keeper's way of life became a part of history.

A Pocketful of Passage recalls the lifestyle of a real family as told by Annie Bowen, whose father, Vern Bowen, served as a Great Lakes lighthouse keeper for many years. From 1933 to 1942 he was assigned to Passage Island. The places, people, and incidents in the story are based on her memories and on factual information from old lighthouse logbooks and other historic records. Every effort was made to include Annie's feelings and attitudes about her home. I have altered the record only by compressing her many memories into the incidents of a single summer.

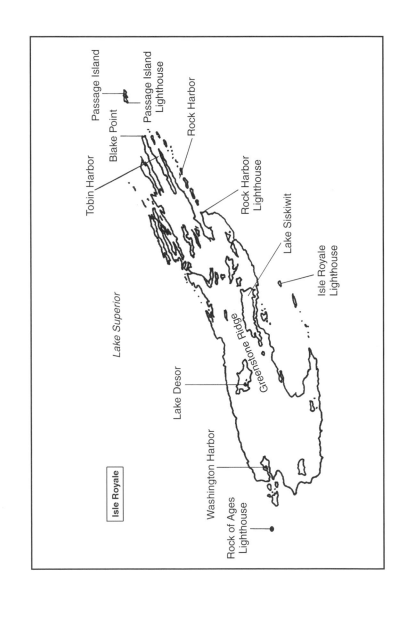

Isle Royale

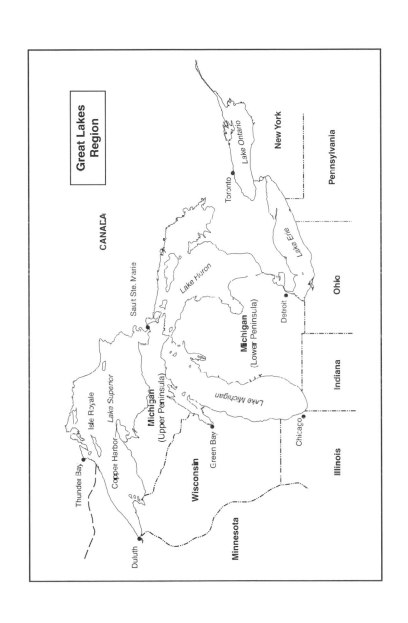

Great Lakes Region

1. Aboard the *Winyah*

I remember that long-ago summer on Passage Island as if it were yesterday. It began, as every summer did, with a midnight boat trip from Duluth, Minnesota. April was always damp and ice cold in the North Country, but I was warm as toast, like a small moth in a snug cocoon. Mama wrapped us in gray woolen blankets to keep off the chilling drafts that crept through the porthole in our cabin. She tucked Jo, Sonny, and me into one narrow berth with

1

wooden sides so that we wouldn't roll onto the floor when the old boat pitched and rolled on giant swells. It was 1942. I was nine and the oldest. Johanna, or Jo, was seven, and Sonny was two. Wedged together and weighed down by the heavy blankets, I could barely move. I couldn't scratch or wiggle, but I didn't care. I was much too excited.

While Jo and Sonny snored, I listened, wide awake, to the drone of the *Winyah*'s engines. She shuddered when she climbed up and over each six-foot wave. Each time she slid down into the trough, my stomach felt like it was riding up and down in an elevator, over and over again. In the next cabin I heard someone upchuck into a bucket. I giggled, proud that I never got seasick. To be completely honest, I loved that all-night roller coaster ride. It took us to my daddy and our summer home at the lighthouse on Passage Island.

Daddy and the other keepers always returned to their stations in early April while the freighters still sat quiet and empty at their winter docks. When the head keeper, Mr. Lane, and Daddy returned to Passage, the harbors and bays were clogged with ice. Two feet of snow blanketed the island. They used pickaxes to hack away the ice that covered the doors to the tower and the fog signal as well as the little tram, a small railroad cart that ran from the dock up to the buildings. Then they cleaned the lamp in the tower, oiled the clockwork that caused the light to flash, and put the fog signal in working order. Within two days, the Passage Light was lit. Each night it pierced the black sky with a bright white beam. The northernmost American beacon on the Great Lakes was ready for the shipping season and the slow parade of vessels that sought safe passage along Isle Royale's rocky shore. It was also time for my mother, who everyone called Billie, and us to join my father.

I woke to the blast of the *Winyah*'s whistle. We had arrived at Washington Harbor, a fishing camp at the western tip of Isle Royale. Jo and I kicked and kicked until the blankets gave way, and we burst from our cocoons. Sonny preferred to play peek-a-boo under the blankets. We'd slept in our flannel shirts and denim overalls, so I was ready and anxious to see the island.

"Breakfast first." Mama's calm but firm voice pulled me back from the door. She reached into her big canvas bag for a dented thermos and a bundle wrapped in wax paper. She poured mugs of chocolaty Ovaltine and unwrapped homemade biscuits spread with butter. Everyone knew my mama made the best southern biscuits. Once a fisherman swapped a whole lake trout for a pan of her biscuits. I ate two biscuits and wiped away my chocolate moustache with Mama's hankie.

"Let's go, Jo!" I puffed as I pulled on my snowsuit, boots, and mittens. Jo licked the butter off her lips. She bit into her second biscuit and shook her head.

"I'm still hungry. Besides it's really cold out there. I'm gonna stay here and play with Sonny."

"You're sure?" I asked.

"Yup."

"OK, but I'm goin'." I always wanted to be outside and couldn't wait to go on deck.

It was a milky morning. Frosty haze drifted over the white ice along the shore. Pearl gray clouds stretched as far as I could see. Snow draped the spires of spruce and fir trees and softened the hard edges of the rocks. It was bitter cold, but the men who hauled crates and barrels from the *Winyah*'s hold didn't seem to notice. They loaded supplies into flat-bottomed fishing skiffs and pulled them like sleds across the shoreline ice to a handful of cabins. In a few short weeks those same small boats would be loaded with nets and rowed out on the lake for the first catch of herring, whitefish, or trout. The men worked fast, exchanging greetings and quick directions. "Ready! Lower away! Watch below!" Their breath escaped in white puffs that froze in icy droplets on their moustaches and stubbly beards.

The *Winyah* stopped at a number of fishing camps along the south shore of Isle Royale before we reached our destination. Each time boxes and bundles of foodstuffs, tools, and supplies were lowered to weather-beaten fishermen who stocked their cabins each spring as they prepared for another fishing season. Mr. Christiansen recorded each item on his clipboard. This enormous man with his big belly and deep voice owned the *Winyah* with his two brothers. Their father had purchased the boat many years ago and had rebuilt it to carry cargo. Few people knew that the grimy and rather top-heavy *Winyah* had once been an elegant yacht owned by multimillionaire Andrew Carnegie.

After he had finished all the paperwork at a stop, Martin Christiansen would holler, "Let her go!" Captain Ole Berg always answered by blowing the whistle. Slowly, the *Winyah* would pull away from the edge of the ice field and continue east along the south shore.

Finally we arrived at Rock Harbor, the last stop of the day. Mama brought Jo and Sonny on deck as the *Winyah* made the slow turn and eased into her berth. We waved and shouted to Daddy who was waiting on the dock.

It was easy to find Vern Bowen in a crowd. He was six feet tall with broad shoulders and thick wavy dark hair combed straight back. Unlike most of the men, Daddy rarely wore a cap. He had sparkling brown Irish eyes and a wide smile. He was dressed in his work clothes: flannel shirt, bib overalls, and a heavy jacket.

The gangplank clanked down. At last I ran off the *Winyah* and into his arms. "Hello, Annie!" he said, scooping me up. In a minute we were all hugging, laughing, and talking. Then Daddy said the words I wanted to hear. "Are you ready to go to Passage Island?"

"Yes!" we shouted in unison.

Within an hour we had loaded the small lighthouse workboat with our suitcases and boxes. I squeezed between a box of canned goods and a twenty-five-pound sack of flour and pressed my nose against a little round window. An icy north wind tossed spray against the glass and filled the lake with whitecaps. It was hard to see through the drops of water, but I kept looking, searching, waiting to see a flash of bright white. Suddenly, I saw it! The white light blinked on, then off, then on again. It was the Passage Island Light. I was home.

2. Magic Carpets on Lake Superior

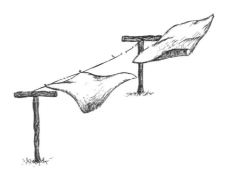

One glorious day in May, the last ice floes on the lake disappeared and spring arrived. Our American flag fluttered on a northwest breeze, letting each passing ship know that we were a United States Coast Guard station and proud to serve our country and the Great Lakes mariners.

I perched cross-legged on the window seat in our bedroom, high above the rocks and the lake. It was a perfect bedroom, except it was painted the same government gray as the other rooms in the house. I always wished the walls were blue. The window was next to the tower and right above the front door of the lighthouse. It was my favorite place to watch the lake and daydream. I imagined soaring off the tower, skimming over the waves like one of the gulls, and landing on the deck of a long, low freighter. Her holds might be filled with iron ore bound for Detroit where trucks and airplanes were built. Or perhaps she carried tons of Canadian wheat headed to flour mills and bakeries in New York City or even across the Atlantic Ocean. I dreamed of sailing through all five Great Lakes and waving to every lighthouse keeper I saw. Then I'd cross the ocean and travel around the world to visit the faraway places they wrote about in *National Geographic* magazine. Someday I might even go all the way to China!

"Annie!" Mama's voice cut my daydream short. She called up from the front yard, "Come back to the kitchen and wash the dishes."

"Yes, Mama," I hollered back, "I'm coming!"

Getting to the kitchen from my second-floor bedroom was not easy. I stepped through the metal passageway between our room and the spiral staircase in the lighthouse tower. Up a half-flight of stairs was the lantern room, where Daddy whistled as he cleaned the brass. His tune filled the tower with sweet sounds. Down one flight was the front entryway to the house. Down and around, down and around—my feet made a hollow clunking sound on the metal stair grates. When I got to the main floor, I ran out the front door and around the house, past the rhubarb patch to the kitchen door. It may seem strange, but our family was not allowed to walk through the house. There was no central hallway, and we were not permitted to walk through the head keeper's bedroom or private sitting room on the main floor. So to get from my family's two bedrooms on the second floor to the kitchen in the rear of the house, we had to go outside.

I pulled open the kitchen door. Warm cinnamon buns! Mama was already there, pulling trays of golden rolls from the oven. "Annie-honey," she called over her shoulder, "please take those mixing bowls to the sink and wash them up. I have to hang the blankets out to dry."

Every spring Mama washed all our blankets and hung them on the clothesline to dry in the fresh air. While the rolls were in the oven, she fed the sopping wet wool through the hand wringer on the washing machine in the corner. "Now don't dally, Annie. When I come in I need to mop the floor, so I want the table cleared and wiped clean."

Obediently, I shaved flakes of soap from a large bar on the sink and added hot water from the tank on the side of our woodstove. Then I dumped the dirty dishes and spoons into the suds. Washing dishes after every meal and whenever Mama baked something was my job. My mother baked so often that she smelled like flour and cinnamon when she hugged us. I loved her rhubarb pie and sugar cookies, but not the endless piles of gooey dishes. But I had learned not to complain or leave dirty smears. If I did, Mama opened the cupboard and pulled out every plate and cup for me to rewash, dry, and put away!

Mama picked up her large wicker laundry basket, grunted softly, and headed out the back door. "Jo, you come with me and mind Sonny."

My sister and I took turns watching our little brother. Beyond our small, grassy yard were jagged rocks that dropped in steep, uneven steps to the ice-cold lake. It was a dangerous place for a two-year-old, so Sonny wore a little leather harness that Daddy had made for him. If he was going to be outside more than a few minutes, Mama hooked a rope from the clothesline to the harness. Safely tethered, my brother toddled back and forth on his leash like a puppy, chewing his fingers like a Milkbone. Then he'd plop down and play with his box of toys. However, my parents also told us that if the wind or a storm came up suddenly, we were to sit on Sonny so he wouldn't blow away!

Mama and Daddy always stressed that it was important for everyone in our family to work together and share responsibilities. Mr. Lane and Daddy took care of the light and the fog signal. Mama kept the house spic-and-span. Jo and I did chores, kept our room neat, and watched Sonny.

Mama carried her basket to the clotheslines behind the house and hung the wet blankets on the lines with wooden clothespins. The morning breeze grew stronger as the day went on until Lake Superior was filled with whitecaps, like lacy ruffles on a deep blue petticoat. The blankets billowed and flapped noisily. Each gust of wind tugged harder and harder at the blankets until they stretched straight out. I finished the kitchen cleanup, pulled on my jacket, and ran out the back door to play.

All of a sudden there was a great gust of wind. The blankets and clothespins tore free from the lines and took to the air! Mama shrieked, "The blankets! Oh m'gosh, my blankets! Vern! Help!"

Sonny let out one joyful squeal just before my sister flopped on top of him so he wouldn't blow away too. Daddy was in the tower, washing the lantern room windows. When he saw the blankets in the air he tipped back his head and howled with laughter. "Let 'em go, Billie—there's nothing you can do!"

I laughed too, clapping my hands with glee. "Look! They're flying carpets!" I shouted into the wind.

Mama ran about the yard, waving her arms frantically as the blankets flew out over the lake, then dropped one by one into the water and went straight to the bottom.

"All gone!" said my sister.

"Me git up!" wheezed Sonny.

That afternoon Daddy radioed the Coast Guard and ordered new blankets, but it took weeks for them to arrive on the lighthouse tender. The tenders were large workboats that brought mail and supplies directly to stations like ours.

I always thought it was funny that these very tough work-boats with black hulls were all named after dainty flowers. The *Amaranth* and *Marigold* served the lighthouses and navigation markers on Lake Superior.

For many days Mama fretted about those blankets and worried about us catching cold. The temperature often dropped below freezing along the north shore of Lake Superior during May. Until new blankets arrived, we wore our clothes and heavy jackets to bed, and Mama covered us with extra clothes. She also made us swallow a second spoonful of cod-liver oil or what she called "spring tonic." It was nasty, smelly stuff, and we all hated it, but no one got the sniffles that spring.

3. Captain Needlenose

Mr. Lane and Daddy sat at the kitchen table early in the morning. They sipped black coffee and reviewed their chore list: clean the brass, wind the clockwork in the tower, paint the back door, overhaul the boat engine, and complete the maintenance check for the fog signal. There was always work to do. Keepers knew their stations must be carefully maintained and ready to respond to an emergency or sudden storm.

"Let's get to it," Mr. Lane said as he emptied his cup with one last swallow.

Daddy stuffed dustcloths in his pockets and put on his soft cobbler apron so he wouldn't scratch any of the brass fittings with his shirt buttons. He picked up a small oil-can to lubricate the gears and moving parts in the lantern room and fog signal, plus a toolbox filled with wrenches, pliers, and various screwdrivers. "I'll be in the tower," he said.

Mr. Lane nodded and went to the radio room to update the logbook. Every day he recorded weather conditions and what he and my father did to maintain the station. He noted any visitors, when he or Daddy went to Isle Royale, and any other important happenings in a large notebook. This logbook was kept in a special cupboard in the wall of the windowless radio room. Daddy told me the windows had been bricked over many years ago to protect the logs and the radio they used for talking to ships and other Coast Guard stations. When pelting rain and high winds rattled the windows in the other rooms until I was sure they would crack, I knew my Daddy was right.

While Mr. Lane worked, the radio hissed, "Passage Island, this is Rock of Ages."

Mr. Lane picked up the microphone and replied, "Rock of Ages, this is Passage Island."

"The *Amaranth* just left here and is headed your way. The inspector is aboard. Just thought you'd like to know."

"Roger and thank you," Mr. Lane replied.

The Coast Guard inspected every light station each year. The inspectors were very thorough and very strict. They checked everything from the top of the tower to the corners behind the woodstove. If something did not work perfectly, was dirty or out of order, the keepers received demerits. Inspections were supposed to be a surprise, but often the lightkeepers at one station radioed the men at the next station so they could be ready.

Mr. Lane ran to the tower door and called up the stairs, "Hey Vern, the inspector's on his way. He'll be here before lunch!"

The Rock of Ages light station was located off the southwest tip of Isle Royale, about fifty-five miles away. Mr. Lane knew that the *Amaranth* would probably dock at Passage Island in about three hours. They would have to work quickly but they would be ready. As the men hurried from the tower to the fog signal to double-check all the equipment, Mama sprang into action. She folded laundry, tidied the kitchen, and checked the cupboards and under the beds. The Coast Guard did not allow clutter.

"Annie, put your slippers away and straighten the pillows on your bed."

"Johanna, be a good girl and sweep the back steps while I straighten the pantry. Oh dear, I think I left a spoon in the sink!"

When we were very sure that everything inside and

outside was shipshape, Mama made us change into good clothes. This was one of the few times Jo and I wore dresses and tied bows in our hair. She washed Sonny's face and hands and had us sit on the front steps with some picture books. "Stay right here while I change," she ordered. "Read your stories and show Sonny the pictures. Do not get dirty and mind your manners when the inspector arrives. Don't say a word, Annie. Do you understand?"

"Yes, ma'am," I said. Last year I had gotten into trouble when I told the inspector that he should not give Passage Light a demerit because the hinge on the back door was loose. "I'll be good," I added.

Daddy and Mr. Lane were on the dock when the tender arrived. They wore their navy blue uniforms, white shirts, and dark ties. Their jackets had brass buttons embossed with a lighthouse tower. The same small lighthouse was also stitched in gold and blue thread on their caps. When my daddy wore his navy blues I thought he was the most handsome man in the world. The men saluted the inspector as he stepped off the gangplank. He was a Coast Guard captain, very tall and pencil-thin and had small, round spectacles perched on his long, narrow nose.

"Captain Needlenose," I thought to myself and tried not to snicker.

We watched silently as he inspected the outside of the house and wrote on his clipboard. Then he put on white cotton gloves and went into the house. He ran his finger over the windowsills and shelves. "Humph," he said.

Then he went into the radio room, read the log entries, and checked all the radio equipment. "Humph," he said.

He inspected the tower, the corners and closets in the bedrooms, and the workbench in the cellar. "Humph," he said.

He peeked inside the cupboards, ran his gloved finger down the stovepipe, and looked closely at the new hinge on the back door. "Humph," he said.

Finally the inspector turned to Mr. Lane. "I'll look at the fog signal next," he said and walked out the back door.

"I think his favorite word is 'Humph!'" I whispered to Jo.

"Sh-h-h!" Mama glared at me.

We sat in the kitchen for a long, long time. Eventually we heard the tender's engines rumble and heard it pull away from the dock. A few minutes later Daddy and Mr. Lane strolled through the kitchen door. "Good work, everyone," Mr. Lane said. "Everything is satisfactory."

"Great," Mama smiled. Then she turned to us. "You can change back into your play clothes now. You were very good."

"In fact, you were so good," Daddy added grinning, "I think we should go on a picnic for supper."

"Can we go to the sea arch?" I asked.

"Yeah!" cheered my sister. "We want to go to the sea arch!"

"I think that would be fun," said Mama.

So she packed ham sandwiches, fruit cocktail, oatmeal cookies, and a thermos of ice tea in a picnic hamper, and Daddy brought the rowboat to the dock. He and Mama sang while he rowed us around the point to a place where the waves had pounded against the cliffs for thousands of years and had worn a hole right through the rock. Wind, ice, and waves continued to enlarge the hole until it formed a giant arch. At the base of the arch was a nice little gravel beach where we spread out an old blanket and ate our supper.

That evening the sky was cloudless and the lake was calm. Far across the lake we could see another rock formation stretched out along the horizon. People called it the Sleeping Giant because it looked like a great man lying on his back with his arms folded across his chest.

"Daddy," I asked while munching on a cookie, "will you tell us the story of the giant?"

"You've heard that story lots of times, Annie."

"I know, but it's one of my favorites, and besides, Sonny doesn't know the story. So will you tell it again, please?"

Daddy smiled and stretched. His Irish eyes twinkled as he spoke. "Long ago a tribe of Indians called the Ojibwa came to Lake Superior and built their village. One day their great spirit, Nanabijou, told them that there was a rich silver mine nearby. The Ojibwa people knew if they found the silver, they could use it to make beautiful things. Then they would be very wealthy and very happy. Nanabijou agreed to show them the mine but first they had to promise that they would never tell the white men where it was. 'If you do,' he warned them, 'terrible things will happen.' The Ojibwa promised that they would tell no one. So what do you think happened?"

"They told someone?" Jo's eyes were big and round.

"Yes, Jo. They did. One day a Sioux scout disguised himself as an Ojibwa warrior. He tricked the Ojibwa, and they showed him the mine. Then the Sioux took some of the silver and told white fur traders how to find the mine."

"And then the terrible thing happened!" I exclaimed. "There was a big storm and the white traders all drowned, and the Great Spirit turned into a stone giant."

Daddy pointed to the rocky headlands along the north shore. "That's the giant, sound asleep. And deep in Lake Superior, buried where no one can find it, is the old silver mine."

"Let's hunt for silver," Jo said picking through the gravel on the beach.

We all knew there was no silver on Passage Island, but we still had fun sifting through the bits of rock to find pretty greenstones, which have delicate star patterns in them. Thousands of greenstones were embedded in the ancient volcanic rocks that formed all of Passage Island and Isle Royale. The same waves that had created the arch had pounded the rocks and broken them into smaller and smaller pieces until the greenstones popped out. That evening I found a nice greenstone and some pretty pebbles. I put them in my pocket.

4. Tadpole Soup

I was always a bit of a tomboy. I preferred overalls to dresses and my hair combed in braids rather than curls and ribbons. I had a doll with a polka-dot dress but rarely played with her. She was too fussy and fragile to take outside, and I loved playing outside! My toys were marbles, a game of jacks, and a worn rag doll that I stuffed down the front of my overalls.

Unfortunately, most of Passage Island was off-limits to Jo and me. Beyond the rocky point where the lighthouse stood was the enchanted forest. Daddy used to say, "That's where the little people live." He explained that the little people were tiny fairies that watched over the wilderness and made sure children like us behaved. If we went into the forest, chased a snowshoe hare, or picked wildflowers, the little people would see us and tell our parents. Although I never saw one clearly, there were many times I was sure one of the little people had darted among the towering fir trees just as the wind blew. They zipped around and under huge slabs of rock when sunlight filtered through the thick spruce boughs and splashed on the forest floor. Everywhere in the forest, shaggy tufts of lichen grew on dead tree branches. Grown-ups called the stuff "Old Man's Beard," but I was sure the wisps of gray were the torn wings of little people.

Every spring Jo and I heard the same lecture from our parents. We could not go into the woods without them. Although the island was only about a mile long, it was a big enough wilderness for two little girls to get lost. A bell hung next to the kitchen door. If Mama rang the bell we must be close enough to reach the back door by the time she counted to ten. But I knew that I had grown at least two inches during the winter. This summer my legs were longer and I could run faster. That meant I could sneak farther into the forest and still get back to the house by the time Mama counted to ten.

My favorite spot was along the cliffs on the north side of the island. There I found a ledge perfectly hidden by elderberry bushes. I lay down with my tummy pressed against the bare rock and scooted right up to the edge. From there, I could look straight down and watch the waves crash against the jumble of rocks fifty feet below me. Sometimes they smacked the shore so hard I felt the spray on my cheeks.

There were also wonderful patches of wildflowers in sunny places on Passage Island. Bluebells sprouted in cracks between the rocks, and great clumps of orange wood lilies seemed to reach for the sun. My family called these lovely blossoms tiger lilies. Jo and I always wanted to pick big bouquets, but Daddy said, "No. The flowers are part of the island, just like the hares, wild birds, and foxes. If you girls pick them, there won't be any seeds for new flowers. The patches will get smaller and smaller until they disappear. And don't think that the little people won't tell us if you two pick them!"

Once in a while, however, Mama did pick a few wilting blossoms for us to make watercolor paints. She put the petals in a jar of water and placed it in the sun. Slowly the water turned a pale shade of blue or orange. Then we dipped our brushes in the colored water and created lovely pictures. Thinking back, our tiger lily paint probably left only the palest wash of color on our paper, but to me, it was the finest paint in the world.

We also had a grand playhouse among the rocks below the house. In our imaginations, the black boulders became furniture in our seaside cottage. A cracked rock with its ends tipped up made a perfect bed. Two scooped out rocks made easy chairs for Jo and me. Patches of orange lichen grew on a shelf of rock. They became the hot burners on our stove.

"I want to be the mother today," Jo announced in the playhouse one morning in June.

"You always get to be the mother," I complained and sat down in a reading chair created by two smooth boulders that were nicely warmed by the sun.

"Well, you always get dibs on the stove," she pouted. I had to admit, I loved to imagine all sorts of wonderful meals simmering on my lichen burners.

"OK," I said, "You be the mother. I'll be the cook. I'm going to the store to buy raisins for cookies." I grabbed my tin pail and climbed over a huge boulder, then slid down the other side. Mama had sewn leather patches on the seats and knees of our favorite pairs of overalls so we wouldn't wear holes in them while climbing and sliding on the rocks.

I found where one rock had cracked and split. The deep gash was filled with water. I squatted down and looked into the little pool hoping to find a few pebbles. I saw something move! I looked again, trying hard not to blink. Again, I saw a little flash. Then another. I got closer. Now I could see dozens of tiny round creatures with wiggly black tails. Tadpoles! The pool was full of tiny black tadpoles.

"These are better than raisins," I thought. I dipped my pail into the pool slowly, carefully. Water and tadpoles streamed into the bucket. I was very careful not to spill any water or pollywogs when I scrambled back over the rocks.

"Whatchya' got?" Jo asked.

"Tadpole soup!" I answered with pride. I set the bucket on the burner and slowly stirred the soup with a driftwood spoon.

"Wow! Look at all of them!" My sister was obviously impressed. "What should we do with them?"

I giggled. "Eat them. After all, this is tadpole soup!"

"Yuck! I'm not gonna eat tadpoles!" Jo said, clamping her hand over her mouth.

"Well, maybe you won't," I said, looking up to the yard where our brother sat under the clothesline playing with a pile of wooden blocks, "but I bet Sonny will."

"Do you really think so?"

"Sure, why not? I bet they're even good for him. They probably have vitamins."

"I don't know, Annie," Jo began.

"Oh, come on," I said carrying my tin pail of soup. "We've got to find a real spoon."

Five minutes later the three of us sat under the clothes-line. "Come on Sonny," I said. "It's time for your lunch. Open wide!" I ladled up a generous spoonful of pond water and three tiny tadpoles. "Here you go." Then I slipped the spoon into his mouth. Water dribbled down his chin, but Sonny slurped up most of it along with the tadpoles. Then he smacked his lips.

"You want some more?" I asked. Jo and I laughed as he swallowed spoonful after spoonful of wiggling tadpoles.

Then Mama came out the back door. "What are you all doing?" she asked sweetly.

"We're giving Sonny his lunch," I said proudly.

"Yeah, Annie says he needs vitamins. She made him soup."

"Really. And what kind of soup did you make, Annie?" Mama bent down to join our party. Then she looked at the spoon just as I slipped it into Sonny's mouth.

"Oh my Lord," Mama exclaimed when she saw one of the tadpoles wiggling on Sonny's pink tongue.

That evening I had to wash every dish in the kitchen cupboard and Jo had to dry them. Sonny had the hiccups.

5. Sky Watchers

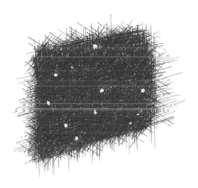

Daddy sniffed the wind and pointed to the dark gray clouds. "Weather's coming," he said, "and it's moving in fast."

Mr. Lane nodded. "Rock of Ages Light Station radioed a few minutes ago. They reported thunderstorms and high winds. We're in for a bit of a blow. I'll close the shutters and start the fog signal. You tend to the boat and the light."

Mr. Lane and Daddy knew weather changed very quickly on Lake Superior. The wind had been dead calm that morning and the lake had been flat as glass at noon. But within an hour, strong west winds churned up enormous waves and a fierce thunderstorm. Quickly, Mr. Lane fastened the heavy wooden shutters to protect the windows. Then he went to the signal.

Many people don't realize that lighthouse keepers also tended fog signals. The rhythmic blasts from these loud horns were very important to ships on the lakes. Mariners listened for the deep "Oouuu-aaawhh!" that could be heard miles away on the blackest night and through the thickest fog.

Mr. Lane knew that visibility got worse when storms arrived. Inside the fog signal building, he shoveled coal into the furnace, which heated the water in the boiler until it turned to steam. When the steam was released through a mechanism called a diaphone, the horn blared! The deafening foghorn blasts bothered most visitors to our island. But lighthouse families were used to the sound. Many nights we fell asleep while the fog signal bellowed.

While Mr. Lane worked at the signal, Daddy checked the ropes that secured our small workboat to the dock. Then he went to light the lamp.

The beautiful lens had an odd name. It was called a Fresnel (FRUH nell) lens after the French scientist who invented it in 1822. It was made of dozens of carefully measured, handcrafted glass prisms placed into a special metal frame. When even a small lamp was lit inside the frame, the light traveled through the prisms, which bent and magnified the rays into a brilliant beam that could be clearly seen by a ship seventeen miles away! For many years lamps burning whale oil or kerosene were used in lighthouses. After 1920, the Coast Guard slowly replaced the old lamps with electric lightbulbs. Passage Light was electrified five years before I was born.

Daddy was always careful not to chip or scratch the prisms when he cleaned them. The smallest crack might reduce the brightness of the beam. Every morning he pulled down canvas shades in the lantern room so that sunlight couldn't travel through the prisms like it does through a magnifying glass. The focused heat from the sun could cause a fire in the lantern room. But when the wind started to howl that hot July day, he raised the shades and turned on the light in the tower. Instantly a beautiful ribbon of glowing white light shot out across the mist and dark green waves. Thunder rumbled.

"Come inside," Mama called. "I'm in the mood for taffy!"

We often made candy when it rained. Many years later, I learned that my mother was very frightened by the fierce storms on Lake Superior. But she never wanted us to be afraid, so she kept herself and us busy making candy when it stormed. It worked. To this day, I love watching storms, smelling the rain, and listening to thunder boom. I also love taffy!

"Jo, would you like to pour the sugar in the kettle?" she asked.

"Yes! Can I stir, too?"

"No, you might burn yourself," Mama said as she added thick corn syrup to the pot. "But you girls can pull the taffy when it's ready." So we watched Mama stir the boiling sugar as rain pounded on the roof. Then she dropped a tiny bit of the hot stuff into a dish of cold water to see if it would form a hard ball. That's a good cook's way of knowing it had boiled long enough and was ready to cool. Lightning flashed! There was a huge clap of thunder. Mama jumped just a bit. Then she hummed a little louder while she worked.

"Annie, get the butter dish and smear a little on your hands and some on Jo's."

This was the best part. Each of us took a wad of warm taffy in our greasy hands. We pulled it into long strips, again and again, until it looked like stiff white satin. The butter kept it from sticking to our fingers. While we pulled, we sang songs and laughed. Outside, sheets of rain fell from the lead gray sky into the dark, churning waves. It was impossible to see across the channel to Isle Royale, but the bright Passage Island Light showed the way. Mr. Lane and Daddy stayed in the radio room until the storm passed, signaling to the men who steered their ships through the passage that stormy afternoon.

By three o'clock the rain stopped. Mr. Lane and Daddy

came to the kitchen table for a cup of coffee and sampled some of the bite-sized morsels of taffy we had wrapped in waxed paper and put in a shallow dish. "Very good," said Mr. Lane. "Why, I think that may be the finest taffy you girls have ever made."

"Thanks, Mr. Lane," I said. "I love making taffy during a thunderstorm."

Mama smiled as she poured herself a cup of coffee. "Looks like it'll be nice and clear tonight," she said.

She was right. That evening there was a golden sunset. Then the sky turned from deep indigo to black with thousands of stars scattered across the heavens like tiny diamonds. There was no moonlight that night, only the beacon in our tower. In the darkness, we listened to the waves swooshing against the rocks. The night air was filled with the scent of balsam fir, spruce needles, and the sweet smell of the lake. Everything always smelled better after a good rain.

"It's a night for sky watching," Mama told us when she gave us "spit baths." The lighthouse did not have a modern bathroom. We had pit toilets in the outhouse and a hand pump at the kitchen sink. Most days, Mama simply filled the kitchen sink with water and washed us with a wet cloth. She always called these spit baths. Once each week we filled the washtub that hung on the back porch and took proper baths. Sometimes, when it was very hot, we went swimming in Lake Superior instead of taking baths.

After our spit baths, we put on our pajamas and brushed our teeth. Mama combed the snarls out of Jo's hair. "Can we stay up really late? Can we, please!" Jo begged.

"I don't know about *really* late," Mama said and gave her a squeeze, "but for a while, as long as you behave and stay on the tram."

"Oh, we'll be good," I said.

The tram was a small wooden cart with grooved wheels that sat on narrow railroad tracks. The tracks ran from the dock up a long rocky incline to the fog signal building. When the tender brought coal, machine parts, and other supplies to the station, the men loaded them onto the tram and then pulled the loaded cart up the hill using chains. When we arrived at the island in early spring and the ground was still covered with ice, we got to ride up the hill on the little tram! It was great fun and much safer than sliding on the ice. But on warm summer nights, the tram served as our patio.

We sat in the dark and looked at the stars, talking in hushed whispers. "See, girls," Daddy said, pointing, "there is the Big Dipper. Those two stars in the bowl point to the North Star—right there! Now, you see that smudge of light across the sky? That's the Milky Way."

My eyes followed his fingertip as he told us about the constellations. Then, all of a sudden, he stopped. He stared at the sky and touched my mother's knee. "Hey, Billie," he said, "do you see that green glow to the north? I think we've got Northern Lights!"

Mama looked and then smiled. "Yes, I see it. I think you're right. Look, kids! Watch over there. Watch closely and you'll see a soft green light. Look, it's getting bigger!"

As my parents spoke the glowing lights did get brighter and bigger. Soon the sky seemed alive with shafts of pink, white, and green that rippled like curtains in the wind. Then, high above our heads the Northern Lights pulsed and danced. Mama and Daddy leaned back on the tram, and Jo, Sonny, and I lay against them. My head rested on Daddy's chest. "So pretty!" I whispered.

"Yes," his voice was slow and hushed. "The world is so beautiful. You must always look for the beauty, Annie. Use all your senses. Don't look at things in black and white. Use your eyes to see in Technicolor. Too often, when people grow up, they start to hurry. They rush so much they miss all the shades of color and all the beauty in this world. Everything, including that storm this afternoon, has beauty if you look for it."

Daddy's voice was as soft and gentle as the night air. See the colors. Find the beauty. These thoughts and the Bible, which they read each day, always guided my parents. I would remember. We watched the lights until our eyes grew heavy and the Northern Lights dimmed. Daddy's words, however, never faded away.

6. Rescue

Great Lakes lights, fog signals, and radio beacons have guided thousands of boats through murky nights and raging storms. Although these navigation aids saved lives over the years, many ships have still been lost. Daddy told us how once the Passage Island keepers helped rescue shipwrecked people.

In December 1906, a wooden steamship called the *Monarch* tried to get to the locks at Sault Ste. Marie during a bad storm. But the ship got lost in the blinding snow and smashed into the rocks just south of Blake Point on Isle Royale. Brave crewmen managed to fasten a lifeline between the sinking ship and the rocks, and the forty-four people on the *Monarch* climbed to shore using the rope. They made a fire on the rocks to keep warm and signal for help.

A Passage Island keeper saw the fire and responded. He rowed alone nearly four miles across the open passage. It took all his strength to keep his small boat from being overturned by the enormous waves. The keeper's face and hands were numb by the time he reached the *Monarch*. But when he saw the people on the rocks he knew that they were nearly frozen. He promised he would get them help. Then the keeper and one of the ship's crew rowed back to Passage Island in the tiny rowboat and relayed news of the stranded survivors to a passing freighter. Finally, two days later, the passengers and crew were rescued.

A dramatic wreck like this one did not occur while my daddy was stationed at Passage Island. However, I do remember how our station helped lost fishermen one very dark, foggy night. For three days the north shore was shrouded in fog. Daddy and Mr. Lane worked around the clock. They took turns tending the fog signal, winding the clockwork in the tower, and monitoring the radio. Mama made them hot coffee and hearty stew, but there was little time to eat.

On the third day, after Sonny, Jo, and I had finished

our supper, Daddy rushed into the kitchen wearing his rain slicker and boots. "Billie, there's a fishing boat out there. She's been lost in all this fog and drizzle. We're bringing 'em in. They're probably pretty wet and hungry." The door slammed and Daddy disappeared into the night.

Within a half hour our little kitchen was full of soaking-wet men. Mama showed them a room where they could take off their wet things and put on Daddy's clothes. Soon there were soggy shirts and dripping trousers hanging everywhere. Mama fed everyone bowls of hot stew, homemade biscuits, hot coffee, and cake. Mr. Lane, Daddy, and the men talked quietly, but no one talked to us, and we did not say a word. When I was young, good children were seen but not heard.

One man with a stubbly beard, however, spoke in a loud voice. He was upset about the fog and because he had lost his pipe. Daddy saw how shaken he was and gave him one of his pipes and a tin of tobacco. "Thank you kindly," the man said gratefully. His fingers trembled as he filled the bowl and struck a match. As he puffed on the pipe, he relaxed and talked more quietly.

A second man looked very cold and frightened. He had pulled a blanket around his shoulders but still shivered. He didn't say anything, but stared into his mug of coffee. Then I noticed tears on his cheeks. I had never seen a man cry before, so this surprised me. I wanted to ask him all about the fog and his boat. I wondered if he had children and was worried about them, or if he thought his boat was going to sink. I wanted to tell him that he was safe at our lighthouse. But I just sat with Jo and Sonny and said nothing. After the table was cleared, Mama took us around the house and up to bed.

"Were those men scared?" I asked, still thinking about the shivering man.

"Yes, some were frightened. It's very scary to be lost on the lake."

"Daddy always says you have to respect the lake when she gets riled up and find a safe harbor," Jo said.

"Your daddy's right," said Mama.

"Was Passage Island a safe harbor tonight?" I asked.

"Yes," she said and kissed us each on the forehead. "Now go to sleep."

As I pulled the blankets up to my chin, I felt safe and warm. I was also very proud of my parents and our lighthouse.

The next morning the weather cleared and the men were able to leave after a hearty breakfast of Mama's pancakes. They all looked much happier and thanked us for the food, warm clothes, and hospitality. One of the fishermen patted Jo and me on the head. He said in a kind voice, "We always see this little lighthouse when we pass by. The next time we come through we'll blow the whistle to say hello." Then he gave each of us a nickel.

"Thank you," we said politely. In 1942, five cents was

quite a bit of money to give a child. Most children were thrilled when given a nickel. However, there was no place to spend five cents on Passage Island, so Mama just put our coins in a jar to spend when we went to the mainland in the winter. Quietly, I wished the man had pulled Hershey Bars, oranges, or comic books out of his pockets. I loved chocolate, fresh fruit, and brand new comic books, but we seldom had those things on Passage Island. All our fruit was canned, and Mama kept hard candies because chocolate melted too easily. So I promised myself that when we got to Copper Harbor I would ask if I could buy a great big chocolate bar.

7. Boat Day

"Time to wake up," Mama nudged us early one morning in August. "It's boat day."

Boat day! Only Christmas or my birthday was more exciting. I elbowed my sister and hopped out of bed. "C'mon Jo! It's boat day!"

"OK, I'm comin'!" she squeaked from under the sheet.

Either Daddy or Mr. Lane went to Isle Royale on boat day, when the *Winyah* arrived with mail, groceries, and any

39

supplies that were not brought directly to Passage by the *Amaranth*. Sometimes our family joined Daddy when it was his turn to spend the day on Isle Royale.

"Get dressed," Mama ordered as she dropped brand-new overalls, cotton shirts, and high-topped sneakers on the bed. She didn't want us looking shabby in old pants with the seats worn thin from playing on the rocks. The new denim was stiff and not nearly as comfortable as our old pants, but we knew better than to whine. Mama insisted that we look neat, clean, and well-dressed when we visited the big island.

"Annie, stop fidgeting! I'm trying to braid your hair." Mama talked while holding a comb with her teeth. I did my best to stop squirming, but it was so hard to hold still when I was excited.

After lots of tugging and pulling, she patted my backside. "All done. Jo, you're next." When she was satisfied that Jo's curls were in place, she smiled and nodded. "All right, girls, let's get downstairs." Mama slung her canvas bag on her shoulder and rested Sonny on her hip as we spiraled down the staircase.

Daddy was already in the lighthouse boat. It was a small, sturdy craft with a central cabin. The engine and steering wheel sat in the middle of this cramped room. On either side of the motor were wooden boxes bolted to the floor. They served as seats for us and as storage chests for life jackets. Outside the rear cabin door was a wooden rudder.

Daddy steered the boat inside the cabin using the wheel or outside with the rudder. Most of the time he stood outside and held the rudder between his feet.

Mama took us inside the cabin and gave us life jackets. They were bulky and smelly, and I hated putting them on, but Jo and I knew we couldn't ride in the boat without wearing them. The only thing that smelled worse than the musty jackets was the stinky boat engine. It reeked of oil, fuel, and exhaust and was quite noisy. But while it did not look or sound very elegant, the tough little lighthouse boat was very important and carefully maintained. It was the lighthouse keeper's primary transportation and served as a rescue boat when there was an emergency on a ship.

Mama sat on one box with Sonny on her lap. Jo and I scrunched together on the other box. "All set, Vern," she called to Daddy, and he eased away from the dock.

We ate breakfast on the boat. Mama had sandwiched fried Spam drizzled with maple syrup between cornmeal patties. On special mornings like this we also had tin cow and coffee. Our family never had fresh milk on Passage Island. The tender brought us cans of evaporated milk that we always called tin cow. It was thick and didn't taste very good but I did like it mixed with a bit of hot coffee. I felt so grown-up when I got to drink coffee.

Daddy sipped from his mug as he steered the boat across Lake Superior toward Blake Point, the ragged tip of Isle Royale. It always amazed me that this lake and the beautiful islands had been made by ice. Thousands of years ago, immense glaciers covered much of North America and all of Michigan. As they inched across the land, they gouged out the Great Lakes and carved the parallel ridges and deep valleys of Isle Royale. Passage Island is part of the Greenstone Ridge, the longest, highest ridge on Isle Royale. The passage between the two islands is a deep gully the glacier scooped out of the ridge.

Daddy slipped into Tobin Harbor just south of Blake Point. Tobin was long, narrow, and beautiful. The forest grew right down to the water's edge, and the massive roots of old fir trees clung to the rocky shore. Their graceful boughs leaned out over the water.

Daddy eased up on the throttle as a bull moose swam across our bow. His big snout and great antlers poked above the waves as he glided through the deep water. When he reached a shallow spot on the opposite side he stood up and looked right at us. Water streamed off his back and massive shoulders.

"Look at him, Mama! He's huge!" I exclaimed.

Local fishermen often joked that moose were made from the spare parts of other animals because their front and back ends don't seem to match. They have very thick necks and broad shoulders to hold up their big heads and heavy antlers. But their hips and rumps are skinny, and their legs look long and spindly. A funny flap of skin called the bell dangles from their necks. Yet as awkward as these animals appear, they are perfectly designed for life in the north woods. Moose are strong swimmers and spend hours standing in cold water where they eat water lilies and pond-weeds. Then they disappear into the woods as quietly as a whisper.

"We'll give him lots of space," Daddy said, pulling up on the throttle. "You never want to upset a moose. That fellow can run up to thirty-five miles per hour!"

My family watched this wonderful animal as he munched on balsam fir, his favorite food. Moose did not live on tiny Passage Island, so seeing one on Isle Royale was always a real treat.

Daddy turned toward the fisherman's wharf and slowed the engine. Putter-put-put, putter-put-put. He leaned against the rudder, pulled alongside the dock, and tossed two ropes to Mr. Johnson, who looped them over wooden cleats. "Hey there, Vern. How are ya?" he asked.

"Just fine, Arnold, and you?"

"Good, good." He shook Daddy's hand when my father stepped onto the dock, then touched his finger to his cap when he saw my mother. "Morning, ma'am." His voice seemed almost musical to me.

Most of the fishermen on Isle Royale were the grown children of parents who emigrated years ago from Finland, Sweden, or Norway. There were also descendants of Cornish miners and a few French and Irish families. These men carried on their family traditions and, like their fathers, caught lake trout and herring. They also spoke like their fathers, with a hint of the old country in their speech.

The dock at Tobin Harbor bustled with activity compared to our isolated lighthouse. Boats came and went. Wives picked up groceries and their mail in a weather-beaten cabin that functioned as a small store. Men pushed and shoved heavy barrels of salted fish into a large warehouse next to it. People exchanged greetings, local gossip, and news of World War II. Grown-ups always talked about the war, but I knew little about it except that my mother was very worried because her two brothers were soldiers. Sometimes when she talked about them her eyes filled with tears.

Just beyond Tobin Harbor and over the hill, Rock Harbor was also busy. During the summer wealthy people from big cities like Detroit and Chicago stayed there at a very nice lodge. These visitors enjoyed the clean northern air, beautiful scenery, fishing, and hiking. However, Tobin Harbor fishermen did not mingle with the tourists unless they were hired as guides, and Daddy made it very clear that we were not to bother the people by the lodge.

Frankly, Jo and I were too busy enjoying the sights, sounds, and smells of Tobin Harbor to pay much attention to any grown-up conversations. We watched men stretch their wet fishing nets on big wooden reels to dry in the sun. One very old man with skin like creased brown leather sat in the shade mending a net. Strands of cotton thread slipped through his gnarled fingers as he tied knots. A long-haired dog sat patiently near his feet. Both Jo and I loved dogs. I held out my hand for him to sniff.

"It's OK for you to pet him," the old man said without looking up. "Amos is gentle."

"Thank you, sir," I said and scooted up beside the dog. Amos promptly rolled over and offered me his belly.

"Hello, boy," I said and scratched his tummy while Jo stroked his head and soft, floppy ears. Amos reached back and licked her face. We both giggled. The three of us enjoyed a fine visit while our parents were busy in the store.

The very best part about the day at Isle Royale was a visit with Pete and Laura Edisen. Their fishing camp was at the end of Rock Harbor, very close to the oldest lighthouse on Isle Royale. The abandoned Rock Harbor Light was originally built to guide ships that transported copper dug out of the early mines on the island. But the copper mines failed, and the lamp in the little white tower had not been lit since 1879.

Everyone knew Pete and Laura Edisen. Pete was kind, funny, a skilled carpenter, and a terrific fisherman. Laura was gentle, sweet, and a wonderful cook. She loved to swap wild thimbleberries that grew on Isle Royale for rhubarb that Mama picked from our patch on Passage Island. Back then children referred to all adults as "Mr." or "Mrs." However, the Edisens were very special friends, and we called them Pete and Laura, not Mr. and Mrs. Edisen.

"Hi, Pete!" I shouted and waved when we reached their dock. Pete sat on a stump dressing the herring he had caught early that morning. He looked up and waved, a big smile on his face.

"Laura," he shouted. "Put on a pot of fresh coffee. The Bowens are here!"

"Tell them they must stay for lunch," Laura hollered back through the little kitchen window.

We did stay and had a fine meal of smoked whitefish, homemade bread with jelly, and canned peas, followed by thimbleberry pie and coffee for dessert. Pete told Daddy that this year's catch was lighter than last year's, but they were doing fine. Laura told Mama all about a lady on the island who had just had another baby. Then we heard something tapping at the door. "What's that?" I asked.

Pete smiled and said with a wink, "That, Annie, is a little friend of mine who's come for his lunch." Everyone on Isle Royale knew that Pete Edisen had a special way with wild animals. People talked about a beaver and a mink that used to come to his fish shack for food.

"What kind of friend?" I asked.

"One that likes fish," said Pete. "Do you want to see him?" Our heads bobbed up and down. "All right," he whispered. "Nice and quiet. We don't want to frighten him."

We all stood up and everyone took care not to scrape chair legs on the wood floor. Pete went to the door and slowly, very slowly, opened it. A beautiful herring gull cocked his head and looked up at Pete with bright yellow eyes.

"Hello, buddy," Pete said in his gentle voice. "You want a nice fish, don't you? Now don't you worry about these folks. They're friends of mine. They won't hurt you." He reached into a bait bucket, pulled out a small fish, and held his hand up high in the air. The gull flew up, turned on outstretched wings, and nabbed the fish from Pete's fingers. The bird swallowed it in one gulp before he landed on the dock.

"You need seconds?" Pete asked holding up a second fish.

Again the gull flew up and snatched the fish. The graceful bird took four more fish before he flew out across the harbor, calling as he went.

For a minute no one said a word. Then Jo whispered, "Wow."

"He started coming by in the spring," Pete said. "Some days he follows me out in the boat. It seems he just wants a few pieces of bait and a little conversation."

"He sure is a pretty thing," Mama said.

"Will he let you pet him, Pete?" I asked.

"Never tried to touch him, Annie. Gulls are wild. I think it's best that we just respect one another. Don't you agree?"

I thought for a minute about the moose and Amos and the gull. "You're right, Pete. We can pet dogs." Then I noticed a small feather on the dock. "Look what he left behind!" I exclaimed and picked up the beautiful gray-tipped feather. "Can I keep this?" I asked.

"Sure," smiled Pete. "You might think about putting it in your hat."

I stroked it with my finger and slid it into my pocket.

It had been a long and wonderful day, but we had to leave. Daddy was on duty that night. So we said goodbye and promised to visit again. Little did we know that our boat ride back to Passage Island would almost end in disaster.

8. Fog

The weather changed quickly, silently, as it often does on Lake Superior. As we made our way home from Isle Royale, cool air moved in over the lake. Within minutes a thin layer of haze formed and turned into a blanket of fog so thick we could not see Blake Point behind us. Far ahead, Daddy could barely see the Passage Light. He listened for the fog signal.

"Don't worry," he said calmly, "We'll get home. But we need to be careful so we don't run into another boat. I want you kids to be very quiet so I can listen."

"Not a word, girls," Mama cautioned us. She rocked my brother, who was fast asleep.

Daddy stopped the boat. He rang the bell to alert any vessel nearby. Then he stretched his neck as far as he could and listened. Nothing. We started to move again very, very slowly. Then he stopped again, rang the bell, and listened. The only sound we heard was the slap of waves against the side of the boat. Daddy repeated the process again and again as we crossed the channel: move forward just a bit, slowly and carefully, ring the bell, then stop and listen.

I had never seen fog so thick. I looked at Mama. Her mouth was a straight line, and I saw the strained muscles in her neck. She rocked back and forth patting my brother's bottom. Then I looked out the little round window. All I could see was white.

Daddy stopped once more. All of a sudden we felt a deep rumble and heard a great swishing sound. Then we saw something big and dark. A huge freighter was about to slam right into us! It seemed as tall as a skyscraper to me. Daddy yanked on the rudder with both hands to turn our boat away from the passing ship. Her wake and the foaming water churned up by her propellers tossed our boat around like a tiny cork. We rocked back and forth so hard I thought we would tip over. Mama grabbed the window ledge to keep from falling. Jo and I landed on the floor. Water gushed over the top of the boat and swirled around our feet. "Hold on!" Daddy yelled, pulling on the rudder.

Mama screamed and started to cry. When Jo saw that Mama was afraid, she started to wail. All this woke up Sonny and he screamed too. I was silent. Perhaps I was too scared to cry. Perhaps I only thought about how big that ship was. But then I looked at Daddy. He was as pale as the fog, and his eyes were wide open and full of fear. The hard knot in my belly crept up into my throat. I couldn't swallow. I couldn't breathe.

"It's OK, Billie. It's OK," he hollered to my mother as he tried to keep us from capsizing. When the violent rocking finally stopped, he rubbed his brow with his fingertips. "It's OK," he said again.

"No, it's not OK, Vern," Mama sobbed. "I can't do this anymore."

I didn't understand what my mother meant. Yes, that ship had almost crushed us. But Daddy had turned us away in time. He knew what to do. We were safe. Besides, it had been such a wonderful day.

No one said a word for the rest of the trip. Soon we could hear the Passage Island fog signal calling to us. We were home.

9. In Trouble

As I got older I developed a real knack for getting into trouble. I wasn't naughty on purpose, just curious and full of energy and imagination. Unfortunately, that summer my imagination continued to get Jo and me into trouble.

One hot summer afternoon there was heavy traffic in the passage. A steady procession of "down bound" freighters headed south and east to the locks at Sault Ste. Marie. Jo and I watched them from our rocky playhouse.

"Hey, let's play mermaid!" I said, recalling a magazine

ad I had seen in the keeper's book box. The Coast Guard always sent portable libraries or book boxes to the remote stations. When the *Amaranth* brought supplies, the crew also delivered a fresh box of books and magazines and took away the old box. I loved *National Geographic* but was never fond of the spelling and arithmetic workbooks they sent.

"How do you play mermaid?" Jo asked.

"Well, first we have to take off our clothes, because mermaids don't wear shorts. Next, we have to climb out on those rocks like we're climbing out of the sea. Then we sit like mermaids on the tip of that rock and wave to the ships. When they see us, they'll blow their whistles!" I pointed to the farthest rock on our point.

"We're not supposed to play out there," Jo said flatly. "We're supposed to stay here on the playhouse rocks."

"I know, but we could see the boats better from that rock, and they could see us. Wouldn't it be neat if they blew their whistles at us?"

"Yeah," Jo nodded her head slowly. "But do you really think we need to be naked?"

"Well, not all the way naked," I said. "You can leave on your underpants." I unbuttoned my shirt and slipped off my sneakers. "C'mon Jo," I urged, "Let's go!"

Within minutes we wore only our underwear. The sun was hot on our skin, but the breeze from the lake was delightfully cool. Then Jo and I climbed very carefully across the jagged rocks. Patches of rough lichen scratched our feet, but where the rocks were bare and wet it was slippery. Waves splashed against the dark stone and poured into the narrow crevices between the boulders.

"That's cold!" shrieked Jo when the spray from a large wave drenched her.

"It feels great! Mermaids love the sea!" I shouted back. "Keep going! We're almost there!"

Finally we could go no farther. We had reached the last exposed rock where the breeze was brisk and the waves pounded against the boulders.

"Sit here," I said, pointing to a flat spot, high above the sparkling water, "and wave to that freighter!"

So Jo and I perched on the rock with our backs to the lighthouse and deep water all around us. We waved and called to an immense freighter probably two miles off the point, certain the captain would see us. He did not. But Daddy did. He was in the lantern room in the tower when he noticed our game. We never heard him come up behind us.

"What do you think you're doing?" His voice was very stern.

I jumped, startled. "Hi, Daddy," I said. Although he didn't sound angry, my father did not look very happy.

"I asked you a question, Annie. What are you doing out on these rocks?"

"Playing mermaid," I whispered and felt my cheeks flush red and hot.

My father squatted down beside us. "Your mother and I have told you many times that these rocks are dangerous. If big waves came in, you'd both be swept away in a second. We'd never find you, Annie. You know how fast weather changes on this lake. You are old enough to know better. I'm disappointed in you." Those words stung worse than a spanking. I never wanted to disappoint my father.

"I'm sorry, Daddy," I said. I stared at my toes, unable to look into his disapproving eyes.

"Me too," said Jo. "It was Annie's idea."

"I'm sure it was," he said and stood up. "And I'm sure neither of you will ever come out here again. Annie, I'm taking Jo back across the rocks. You stay put. I'll be back for you in a minute." As he spoke, Daddy scooped up my sister. Then he turned and made his way back to solid ground. Tears welled up in my eyes while he was gone. I rubbed them away with the back of my hand. Moments later I heard his boots scrape against the stone.

"Come on, Annie," he said taking my hand. "Let's go." As we climbed over the rocks, Daddy asked one more question. "Have you any idea how upset your mother would be if she had seen you out there?" Neither of us answered out loud, but I thought about this a lot.

I never played on those rocks again, but near the end

of that summer I managed to get into worse trouble. Mr. Lane's wife, his son Larry, and his nephew Peter came for a visit in late August. They never stayed on Passage Island for more than a few weeks each summer, but I was always happy when they arrived and we had playmates. The boys were about my age, but taller and faster. They liked tag, baseball, and exploring. Every day with Larry and Peter was great fun and an adventure.

One morning Jo, the boys, and I slipped into the woods along the north side of the island. We followed the path beyond my favorite ledge to another spot where you could see straight down to the rocks and water far below. Larry had sharp eyes and noticed a bird's nest tucked into a notch in the rock, about ten feet below us. All the nestlings had fledged weeks before, but one unhatched egg remained in the nest.

"Wow, look at that!" Larry exclaimed. "There's still an egg in that nest. I wonder if we could get it. Maybe it would hatch!"

"I dunno," Peter said and wrinkled up his nose. "That egg's been sitting in the sun all summer. I bet it's really rotten inside. But," he added with a grin, "it would be neat to have the nest."

"Sure would," Larry agreed. "I think we could get it if we had some rope."

I knew where Daddy and Mr. Lane kept a rope in the fog signal building. The fog signal was off-limits for children, but the coiled rope hung on a hook just inside the door. I hesitated for only a second. "I know where there's a rope," I said proudly.

"Let's go!" said the boys.

We ran back to the lighthouse. There were no adults in the yard so I slipped into the fog signal building and grabbed the rope. "This will work great," said Larry. "It's strong and plenty long."

I don't remember how we decided that Larry would be the one lowered over the side of the cliff to get the nest. We tied the rope around his waist with a double knot. Then Jo, Peter, and I hung on to the rope as Larry climbed down over the edge. Peter stood closest to the cliff and braced his foot against a stone. I stood next in line and Jo stood behind me. We let the rope out hand over hand. Larry was heavier than I had imagined. It took all our strength to keep the rope from slipping. Then Larry shouted, "OK, I got it! I got the nest! Pull me up!"

"All together," Peter commanded. "*Pull!*"

We yanked at the rope and pulled as hard as we could. The muscles in Peter's back, arms, and legs tensed and strained. The rope fibers dug into my hands. I tugged with Peter. Behind me, Jo huffed and puffed. But we were not strong enough to pull Larry back up. He dangled fifty feet above sharp rocks and pounding waves, gripping the rope with one hand and clutching the nest with the other.

"Hey, you guys!" he shouted, "Pull me up!"

"We're trying!" Peter hollered back. Beads of sweat formed on his forehead. "But you're awful heavy!"

I grunted as the rope dug into my hands. "I don't think we can pull him up!"

"What are we gonna do?" Jo started to panic and cry.

"Don't cry!" Peter demanded. "Don't be a sissy!"

"Well, we've got to do something!" I said. My hands burned and my arms hurt.

"I guess one of us has to go for help." Peter sounded scared too.

That's when I panicked. I thought of Mama and Daddy finding us in the woods, where we were not allowed to play, with a rope we had stolen, to get a bird's nest we were not allowed to have. Then fear grew into horror. What if Larry fell? What if the rope broke, or we let go and Mr. and Mrs. Lane's son fell to his death? Would our parents ever forgive us?

"I think you're right," I said. "I think you should go."

"OK, but you girls can't drop him when I let go."

"We won't," I said trying to sound tough. "Jo and I are strong."

"I don't know!" Jo cried.

"Yes, we are!" I shouted to Jo, but I was really trying to convince myself. "Hurry up, Peter! Run and get help."

When Peter let go of the rope, it was all Jo and I could do to keep from sliding over the edge. My feet skidded on loose stones as I fought to brace myself as he had. I had never been so frightened. Each second seemed like an hour. Sweat trickled down my neck. A fly buzzed around my head. My shoulders, arms, and legs ached and my hands burned. There was a tight knot in my tummy and a worse feeling down below when I realized how much I needed to pee. But I concentrated, and I forced Jo to concentrate. "Hang on," I shrieked to her. "Don't let the rope slip! Don't drop Larry!"

"Hey, somebody pull me up!" Larry yelled.

"Hang on," I shouted back. "Peter's gone for help!"

"Oh no!" Larry wailed. "They're gonna kill us!"

Finally I heard voices and footsteps on gravel. My father, mother, Larry's mother, and Peter rushed up the path. At the same time, far below us, Mr. Lane came around the point in the rowboat. Quickly he positioned the boat among the treacherous rocks in case his son fell and needed to be rescued from the lake.

Daddy brushed me aside. "Give me that!" he demanded and grabbed the rope out of my hands.

"Let's pull him up!" he called to the women. Together they struggled because the rope was snagged on twigs and wedged between cracks in the rock. It took a lot of work to pull Larry up and out of harm's way.

"We've got him," Daddy shouted down to Mr. Lane when he finally gripped Larry by the seat of his pants and yanked him up over the edge.

I was relieved but angry when I saw that Larry still held

the nest in his clenched fist. If he had dropped it, I thought, he might have climbed up the cliff by himself. Our parents would never have known. But there he stood, clutching the nest while his mother cried and hugged him. I looked from Mrs. Lane to Mama and Daddy. My parents glared at Jo and me. They were furious! "Oh no," I thought. But before I could say anything, I realized my pants and shoes were quite soggy. Amid all the excitement, I had wet my pants.

"March!" Daddy commanded and pointed toward the lighthouse path.

"This minute," Mrs. Lane echoed my father's order. Reassured that Larry was safe and unharmed, she was horribly mad at her son and Peter.

The walk back to the lighthouse was silent except for the rhythmic squish of my wet shoes. That afternoon we all received spankings and stern lectures. "You must never, ever endanger a person's life," Daddy concluded his speech to Jo and me in a sober voice. Then Mama sent us to our room.

That night Mama and Daddy talked in their bedroom. It was very late and very dark. I knew eavesdropping was also wrong, but I couldn't help overhear a few muffled words through the partially opened door. Mama's voice was strained, like the day we crossed the passage in the fog. "Enough is enough . . . " she said. "Children getting bigger . . . island's too small . . . too much danger . . . safer playgrounds . . . good schools."

Then I heard Daddy's voice, deep and comforting. "OK, Billie." Next I heard a new word I didn't quite understand.

"I'll transfer," he said. Then it was quiet. They stopped talking and I fell asleep. It had been a long, long day.

The next morning Mrs. Lane packed her bags. Mr. Lane took her and the boys to Isle Royale where they caught a boat back to the mainland. Jo and I watched Larry and Peter leave from our window seat. They looked very glum when they boarded the lighthouse boat. I never saw either of them again.

10. Change

September brought change. The air turned cool. Crisp winds whipped Lake Superior into frothy whitecaps. Daddy and Mr. Lane cut lots of wood for the cookstove and stacked it in the basement. Mama made me recite my multiplication tables every day, and Jo had to work on addition and subtraction problems. We took turns spelling words while we washed the dishes. Every afternoon we sat at the kitchen table, pencils in hand, and toiled over the workbooks provided in the book boxes.

"You must be ready for school when we go to the mainland," Mama said. Usually we left Passage Island in mid-September and went to Duluth, Minnesota, or Copper Harbor, Michigan, for the winter. I liked winter in Copper Harbor best. This village at the tip of Michigan's Keweenaw Peninsula was a tiny, friendly community of families whose lives were tied to the lake. They fished, made and repaired boats, and rented cabins to summer visitors. Their weatherworn homes and shops reminded me of Tobin Harbor. In Copper Harbor Daddy helped build boats and repair engines. He was a jack-of-all-trades and seemed to find work easily.

Although my mother, brother, sister, and I left Passage Island each September, Daddy had to stay behind. The Great Lakes keepers assigned to remote, offshore lights remained at their stations until the end of the shipping season in early December. When ice blocked the shipping channels and the freighters returned to their winter berths, the men "laid up" the stations to make them ready for winter. Daddy and Mr. Lane stored the lighthouse boat and the rowboats in a small boathouse. They drained the boiler in the fog signal and emptied the fuel from the gasoline engines and diesel generators that powered their equipment. They put up storm shutters on all the windows to protect the buildings and the precious lens in the tower. With their work done, they awaited a tugboat that picked them up when weather permitted.

"I don't want to go to school!" I thought as I chewed the end of my pencil. Although I enjoyed learning, children in school called me the dumb lighthouse kid. I was a chatterbox and forgot to raise my hand before speaking. I also had a tough time making friends because we started the school year a bit late, left early, and then disappeared for the summer. While I did well enough in the subjects I learned in the workbooks, I lagged behind in other classes. The thought of entering a stuffy classroom with boys and girls I didn't know made my tummy hurt. Besides, I loved living on the island. So you cannot imagine how I felt the evening when Mama and Daddy told us we were leaving Passage Island forever.

"In the spring we're going to a different lighthouse on the mainland," Daddy explained. "We'll still live by the water, but we'll be able to drive to town."

"You can ride bicycles and roller skate, play with other children, and make real friends. There are stores and a nice school nearby!" Mama added happily.

I couldn't believe what they were saying! Not come back to Passage? Leave my playhouse rocks and secret lookout on the cliff? Never see Pete and Laura again? Never sit in my very own window seat?

"But—but what about Passage?" I stumbled over the words. "Who will take care of this light?"

"A new assistant keeper will move here," Daddy said.

"But this is our light," I insisted. "I want to stay here!

I want to come back here so *we* can take care of Passage Island! This is *our* lighthouse!"

"Annie," Daddy said gently, "you mustn't worry about Passage. The Coast Guard takes care of all the lights. It's time for our family to move to a better place."

Better? What could be better than our beautiful island? But I was nine years old. I did not understand how difficult it had been for Mama to care for three growing children on a tiny island so far from towns with doctors, real stores, churches, and schools. I saw Passage as a wonderland of woods, rocks, and breathtaking cliffs. But my parents saw the dangers as well as the beauty. They saw that every summer their children grew more curious and daring and got into more trouble. Next summer Sonny would be too big for his harness. He would no longer be content to play under the clothesline but would still be too small to play with us on the rocks. My mother was also tired of Lake Superior. While I thought those long boat rides through heavy seas and fog were great adventures, she feared for our lives.

"No, Daddy!" I exclaimed. "I don't want to leave Passage!"

"Annie, that's enough." Daddy's voice was firm. "Now go to your room."

"Stop crying," Jo comforted me. "It'll be OK."

To be very honest, my sister Jo was happy that we were moving. She looked forward to living permanently on the mainland near a bigger town with more friends. Even today she remembers Passage Island as a lonely place, too far from the rest of the world. Her memories of Passage Island are very different from mine.

I ran up the tower steps, curled up in my window seat and stared through the glass at the overcast sky and gray-green water. Colors and shapes blurred with my tears. I couldn't see. I couldn't think. I could not imagine leaving this lighthouse—my lighthouse—forever. Perhaps it was a mistake. Maybe the Coast Guard would send a radio message tomorrow: Vern Bowen and his family are needed at Passage Island. I tried to imagine it was just a bad dream.

But the next morning Mama whistled merrily as she imagined improved keeper's quarters. A modern gas stove, indoor plumbing with hot as well as cold running water, and a real bathtub would make daily life so much easier.

"Annie and Jo," she said as she dished up bowls of oatmeal. "I want each of you to help pack your summer clothes and toys today. We'll be taking them with us this time." Normally we left our lightweight shirts, sneakers, and playthings in a box in the basement. I realized then that this wasn't a dream. We were not coming back to Passage Island next spring.

I remember how hard it seemed to move that morning. My arms and legs felt heavy, like someone had tied rocks to my wrists and ankles. I trudged up the stairs with my cardboard box. I pulled and tugged at the stubborn dresser drawer. Then I thought and thought as I slowly filled the

box. When our belongings were packed and put aboard the
Amaranth, no one would remember that I had ever been
there. Daddy's name was written in the logbooks. But no
one would ever know that Annie Bowen lived here and that
she loved and cared about Passage Island. Suddenly, I knew
what I had to do.

The heavy gloomy feeling disappeared as I ran down
the stairs and found my father carrying an armload of wood
to the basement. "Daddy, can I have another box?" I asked.

"Another box? Can't you fit everything into the one
Mama gave you this morning?"

"Pretty much. I don't need a big box. Just a little one
that's real strong," I said and followed him down into the
cool cellar. Daddy dropped the wood and stacked the pieces
neatly on top of the growing wood supply for the next season. He looked at me quizzically.

"Annie, what are you up to? You're not in trouble again,
are you?" he asked.

"Oh no!" I said. "I just need something to put my treasures in so they don't get broken."

"I see." He sighed, stretched, and rubbed his shoulder.
"Well, I think there's an old tin box on that bench. Some
parts came in it last month, but nobody's used it since then.
You can have it."

On the corner of the tidy workbench was a metal box
with wood trim and metal clamps that held the lid in place.
It was the size and shape of a shoebox. I examined it care-

fully. There were no dents or rust. "Thanks, Daddy!" I exclaimed. "This is perfect."

I turned on my heel and raced back up the basement steps, up the metal spiral, and into my room. After all my clothes were neatly stacked in the cardboard box, I put all my toys on the bed. I had two dolls. Both were named Katherine or Katie because I liked that name. One was my fussy doll with the polka-dot dress, and the other was the beat-up rag doll I had shoved down the front of my bib overalls and played with on the rocks. Her penciled-on face was nearly worn away. I put the ragged Katie in the box with my clothes and squeezed fancy Katie into the metal box. Then I found the bent spoon I had used to feed Sonny tadpole soup and slipped it in the box next to fancy Katie. My ball and jacks and box of crayons went in the clothes box. My bag of marbles went into the metal box. Then I picked up one of my pictures painted with flower petal paints. I printed my name in the corner using my best penmanship, folded the paper carefully, and laid it on top of fancy Katie. The little metal box was full. I closed it and snapped down the clamps on the lid.

When I carried the box outside, the yard was deserted. Mama, Jo, and Sonny were in the kitchen baking sugar cookies. I heard Sonny banging a spoon on the table. Daddy was still in the basement, and Mr. Lane had gone to Isle Royale on business. I found a small shovel in the work shed and tiptoed to the back corner of our yard, where there were patches of grass, clumps of bushes, and some bare soil. It was hard to find a spot in the rocky ground deep enough to dig in and that I could find years later. It took a long time and a few test holes, but eventually I found the perfect spot. Again and again I jabbed the blade into the ground and scooped out shovelful after shovelful of dirt. Finally satisfied that I had dug deep enough, I knelt down, wedged the metal box into the hole and pulled the loose dirt over the lid with my hands. I smoothed the soil carefully. "There," I said to myself as I patted the dirt. "Part of me will stay on Passage Island forever. And someday if somebody finds my toys, they will know that Annie Bowen was here."

That afternoon the *Amaranth* sent a radio message. The tender would arrive at Passage Island the next morning with additional firewood. She would also pick up the assistant keeper's family and transport them to Copper Harbor.

Just before supper, I put on my jacket and slipped silently out the kitchen door. The temperature had dropped, and it was chilly. The cloudy sky was shades of gray, like someone had dusted snow-white cotton balls with soot. All around me Lake Superior roared. Choppy seas smacked the shoreline. Whitecaps pounded our mermaid's perch. "We are leaving. We are leaving." Those words filled my head as the rhythm of the lake filled my ears.

I scooted down over the jumble of damp stone that was

my playhouse. The rocks were cold, but my stove burners still glowed bright orange. I said goodbye.

Next I went to my favorite overlook. I lay down on my belly, peered over the edge, and sucked in the cold, damp air. People always talk about the wonderful smell of salty air near the ocean. But to me, the best perfume is the sweet smell of the Great Lakes. Then I looked across the water. That day the Sleeping Giant was a gray smudge on the horizon. I said goodbye.

Finally I went up the spiral staircase and curled up in my window seat. I tried to imagine another girl or boy moving into my room next summer and sitting in my window seat, but I couldn't.

11. A Pocketful of Passage

The *Amaranth* arrived as scheduled. Piles of wood were transferred from the ship to the dock while the captain and Mr. Lane discussed the weather, the war, and the latest Coast Guard news. Daddy put our boxes on the tender. Then he hugged and kissed each of us. "Be good and listen to your mother," he said. "I'll see you in December!"

Then Daddy hugged Mama and whispered in her ear. She smiled and whispered something to him. "You folks ready?" the captain asked, glancing at his watch.

"All set," Daddy replied. Mama led us up the short gangplank, and Daddy stayed on the dock. It was hard to leave Daddy, but I knew we would see him again. However, this was the last time I would see Passage Island. I looked at the stone lighthouse and the wonderful tower, our tram, the rocks and trees. "Remember all the colors," I thought. "Remember."

The engine rumbled and the *Amaranth* eased away from the dock. I started to cry. Big silent tears ran down my face and dripped off my chin. I wiped them away with the back of my hand, but it was no use. I couldn't stop crying. I tried to look back at the island, to see it one last time, but the ship rocked crazily as she plowed through the rough water and I fell against the rail.

"Come inside, Annie," Mama shouted. "Come inside right now or you'll get washed overboard!"

I obeyed, and I stumbled into the cabin because it was hard to see through my tears. Mama sat on a bench with one arm around Jo and the other cradling Sonny. I wanted to be alone and slumped down on a bench at the other end of the room. My nose was running, so I reached into my jacket pocket for a hankie. Empty. Maybe it was in my overalls pocket, I thought. So I stuck my hand into the pocket next to my leg. No hankie, but I felt other things. My fingers curled around them and gently pulled them out. In the palm of my hand were things I had collected during the summer: some pebbles, a greenstone, a bit of string, and a soft white feather with a gray tip. The feather was tattered because it had been in my pocket ever since Pete's gull had dropped it on his dock. I didn't care. When I saw it I couldn't help but smile through my tears. I stroked it with my finger and remembered that exciting day. Gently, very gently, I slipped these bits and pieces back in my pocket and thought for a long, silent minute. I had left a bit of myself buried in a small tin box behind the lighthouse on Passage Island. But I had taken away a pocketful of Passage. I had a bit of the island with me. These treasures and the memories of my favorite lighthouse were mine to keep forever.

Postscript

In 1943 Annie Bowen and her family moved to the Presque Isle Light on Lake Huron. The name Presque Isle means "almost an island" in French. The tall white tower and snug keeper's house stood on the end of a skinny peninsula that jutted out into Lake Huron just north of the town of Alpena. The Bowens lived at Presque Isle for three years. Annie was happy there and has wonderful memories of life at this Lake Huron station. Sadly, Vern Bowen was seriously injured when he fell off the roof of the fog signal building in 1947. Billie and the children had to leave the lighthouse while he recuperated in the hospital. When he recovered, they moved to Sault Ste. Marie where he worked in the Coast Guard offices. Two years later Vern Bowen retired, and the family settled in Kalamazoo, Michigan.

After she graduated from high school, Annie Bowen married and had a son and a daughter. Years later she fulfilled a lifelong dream and became a nurse. She cared for cancer patients who loved her friendly outlook and gentle ways. After she retired, Annie visited many schools and told children about lighthouses and her childhood memories.

In 1978 the Coast Guard installed a solar-powered signal in the Passage Island tower and replaced the beautiful Fresnel lens with modern plastic optics. The beautiful old lens is now on display at the Coast Guard station at Dollar Bay in Houghton, Michigan. The Passage Light still guides ships, but no one lives on the island. The tram tracks have rusted, and the buildings are boarded up against Lake Superior's harsh weather. Passage Island is now part of Isle Royale National Park. Park visitors can take a small boat to the island and hike through the enchanted forest up to the lighthouse.

Annie did return to Passage Island three times, once with her son and his family. She raised an American flag when they arrived and played with her grandchildren among the rocks, where the lichen burners still glow brightly. She also found the spot where she buried her toys, but she did not dig them up. "They are part of the island," Annie said.

Passage Island always remained her favorite place. Annie passed away in 2006, but hopefully her memories will live on for many years.

About the Author

Loraine (Rainy) Campbell is a naturalist and museum director who loves the Great Lakes. She met Annie Bowen Hoge after leading a Michigan Audubon Society tour to Isle Royale and Passage Island. She lives in Rochester Hills, Michigan, with her husband and their menagerie. This is her first book.

About the Illustrator

Marie L. Campbell is an artist studying at Northern Michigan University, where she hikes the Lake Superior shore with her beloved Saint Bernard. This book is her first collaboration with her mother.